CONTENTS

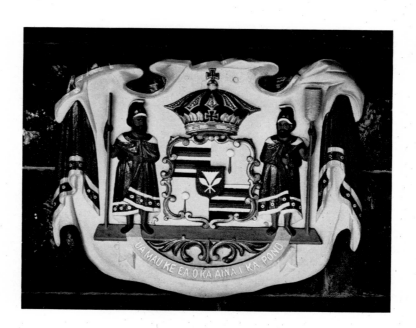

Coat of arms of the kingdom of Hawaii at the
Royal Mausoleum, Honolulu

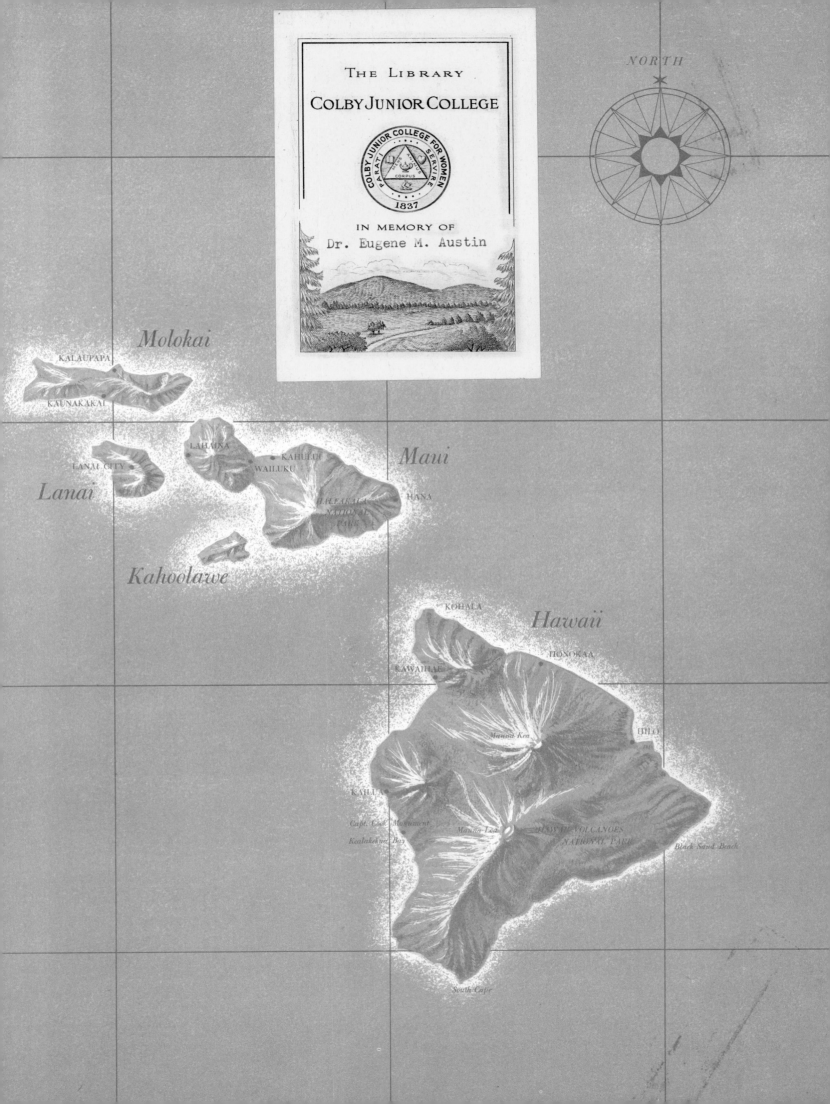

NORTH

Molokai

KALAUPAPA

KAUNAKAKAI

Lanai

LANAI CITY

LAHAINA

KAHULUI
WAILUKU

Maui

HANA

HALEAKALA
NATIONAL
PARK

Kahoolawe

KOHALA

Hawaii

KAWAIHAE

HONOKAA

Mauna Kea

HILO

KAILUA

Capt. Cook Monument

Kealakekua Bay

Mauna Loa

HAW II VOLCANOES
NATIONAL PARK

Black Sand Beach

South Cape

An Introduction to HAWAII

An Introduction to
HAWAII

Photography by
ANSEL ADAMS

Narrative by
EDWARD JOESTING

Published by 5 ASSOCIATES San Francisco

← *Waimea Canyon, Kauai*
(See additional color plates starting on page 59)

Dedicated to Virginia and Harriette

ACKNOWLEDGMENTS

The kind assistance of many people and organizations made this book possible. We are indebted to Joseph Feher, artist-historian of the Bishop Museum in Honolulu, for his careful reading of the text; to Roland Meyer of H. S. Crocker Co., Inc., San Francisco, for his organizing ability and encouragement; and to many other individuals who were so helpful in the securing and production of the photographs.

Acknowledgments are warmly extended to the United States Department of the Interior and the National Park Service for their invaluable help in the photography of Hawaii and Haleakala National Parks, and to the John Simon Guggenheim Memorial Foundation, who granted a Fellowship for the purpose of photographing the National Parks and Monuments of the continental United States, Alaska and Hawaii.

Without the permission of First National Bank of Hawaii this volume would not have been possible. A number of the photographs in the book were made during a photographic project undertaken for the bank on the occasion of their one hundredth anniversary in 1958. The bank's willingness to make these photographs available to the public through this volume is greatly appreciated.

Finally, we are indebted to the Matson Navigation Company for their kind permission to use certain color photographs made during an assignment for them.

FOREWORD

Hawaii is not one of the larger States of the Union, but it is certainly one of the most complicated and fascinating. To tell the full story of these islands in a single volume would be presumptuous indeed. Rather than attempt an admittedly impossible task, we have decided here to explore two vistas of this island State.

One vista is the natural beauty of Hawaii as revealed in black and white and color photographs. To give a balanced impression of the islands is most difficult, because the extremes of scene and mood run from the desolate dry crater of Haleakala to the dense green windward jungles which slope off into the sea. Just as important as the broad views are the myriad details, some the marks and relics of man accumulated over the centuries, which have now weathered and blended with the landscape and magic of Hawaii.

It has been an exacting task to select the sixty-odd photographs which appear in this volume from the large number made over the years. But time has brought a certain selective understanding and appreciation of work accomplished, and this collection seems to represent best that strange combination of wildness and softness, vast space and intimacy, which is the beauty of Hawaii.

This then is the mood and substance of the islands as seen through the eyes of one man. It is a statement of one man's feeling about the land and the vast seas which surround Hawaii.

The second vista explored here is the story of the island people and how they were drawn in successive waves to the shores of Hawaii. The first settlers were the dauntless Polynesians. They lived for centuries in near isolation and their lives were shaped by the bounty and danger of the land and sea.

Hawaiian petroglyph, near Kawaihae,
west coast of Hawaii

Then Captain Cook arrived and the rest of the world soon knew about these islands. Adventurers, missionaries, laborers, businessmen, came in a rush. They mingled with those already rooted in Hawaii. A mixing of people took place, often reluctantly, but it resulted in shared ideas and customs. In the end a unique civilization came forth.

So often reality has been filtered out of history. If this narrative re-creates a little of the urgency and devotion felt by those who shaped Hawaii's past it will have served its purpose.

Our book is only an introduction to the islands. We have intentionally avoided discussion and treatment of the vast contemporary enterprise—cultural, financial and industrial—for such would comprise the subject of a separate literary and pictorial effort. The intent of the photographs and words herein is to move the reader to seek for himself the wealth of natural beauty and discover the rich heritage of the people who make up Hawaii.

ANSEL ADAMS
EDWARD JOESTING

San Francisco and Honolulu
March, 1964

Wave and clouds, east shore of Lanai

*Cliffs and surf in
the late afternoon,
Hanakapiai, north
shore of Kauai*

10

Poi pounder and a small ancient Hawaiian household god

AN INTRODUCTION TO HAWAII

by Edward Joesting

A thousand years before Christopher Columbus ventured across the Atlantic Ocean, Polynesian sailors in the Pacific had already traveled the 2,000 miles of open sea which separates Hawaii from the Society and Marquesas island groups in the south.

The vessels in which these hardy people sailed were great double-hulled canoes, up to seventy feet long, about the size of the PINTA, Columbus' smallest ship. A voyaging canoe could carry a hundred Polynesians together with provisions for a month at sea. A platform connected the twin hulls and here, in a small thatched hut, lived the women and children. On a mound of earth they built fires and cooked their food.

How the first immigrants came

Building an ocean going canoe was surrounded by solemn religious ceremonies. It began in the forest where the tallest koa trees were selected, then felled and hollowed with stone adzes. Planks were carefully hewn and fitted along the top of the hulls as protection against high seas. As the planks were lashed into place with strong braided sennit, workmen chanted a hymn asking divine help to make the lashings strong so that the canoe "may go over short waves and long waves to reach near horizons and far-off horizons." The sweeping bow and stern often carried the carved images of gods, protection for sailors on their voyages. The completed ship, launched amidst chanted blessings, was a masterpiece of grace and beauty.

Building canoes

The canoes moved swiftly through the sea, propelled by the paddles of sturdy bronze-colored sailors and by a plaited mat sail, rigged from the center platform. The voyagers navigated by the stars, by the winds and the currents. Perhaps they were also guided by flights of golden plover. birds which still fly

13

from Alaska to Hawaii and on to the islands in the south, returning each year to their Alaskan homes in summer time.

When they came We can only guess what circumstances brought the first Polynesians to Hawaii. One ancient legend says the islands were first seen by fishermen whose canoe had been driven into unknown seas by a violent storm. Or perhaps a band of men and women were forced from their home islands and in searching for new lands in which to settle, discovered the vast islands of Hawaii. They might have come as early as the first century after Christ, but certainly they were well settled by 500 A. D.

Historians say those first immigrants probably waded ashore through the white surf, onto the black lava rock which divides the sea from the land along the south coast of the largest island, which today is called Hawaii. These sailors must have been awed by the great 13,680-foot peak of Mauna Loa, where perhaps, they saw a mysterious patch of glistening snow.

Ancient Hawaiians believed these favored islands could only *Creation of the islands* have been born of the gods. Old chants say that as the children of certain gods were born they dropped into the the sea, forming the islands of Hawaii. When no more children were born, the creation of the islands was complete. In later times the great chiefs of Hawaii traced their lineage to these gods.

Modern geologists believe the island chain came into being over millions of years of time. Slowly, ever so slowly, lava poured forth from a rift in the floor of the Pacific and steadily pushed upward to the surface against the terrific weight of the great ocean. With more millions of years, other islands appeared along the rift line. Today the islands of Hawaii stretch for some 1,500 miles across the Pacific.

When the islands were new they were naked, harsh domes of lava rock, without insect or plant life. The level of the sea rose and fell. Heavy rains created rivers which rubbed away at the smooth hillsides, eventually forming valleys. Sun and

14

Lava flow with Mauna Loa in background, central Hawaii

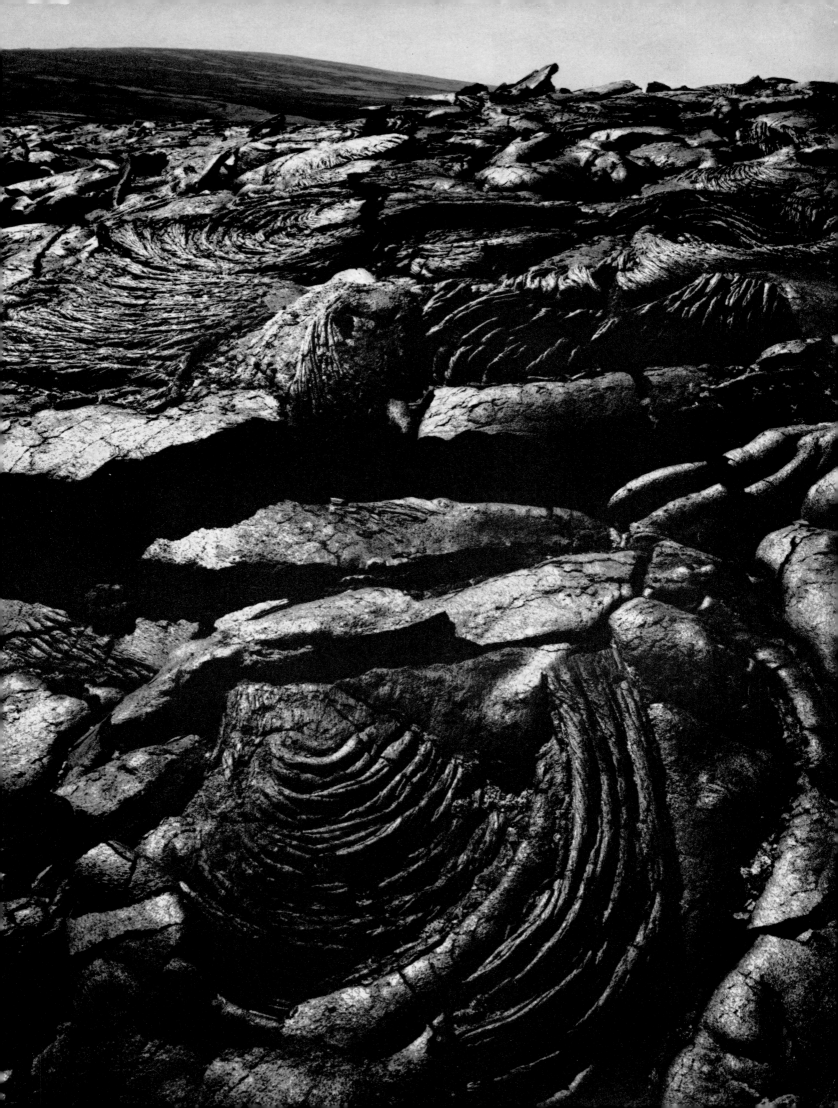

wind worked relentlessly on the basalt rock, which deteriorated with the measured pace of nature.

Nature, in its unhurried way, did bring life to Hawaii, but at the rate of one new specie every 20,000 or 30,000 years. Insects and plant seeds arrived in the plumage of birds which alighted in the islands after flying thousands of miles from other shores. Some forms of life were cast ashore in the trunks of trees or bushes which had been uprooted during storms in distant lands. Still other minute insects and seeds drifted on the upper air currents and landed by chance at some spot where life could be sustained.

The first plants and insects

The plants and insects thrived. There were few enemies to destroy them and they multiplied in the hills and valleys, producing species found nowhere else in the world. The first Polynesians who came ashore stepped into a natural museum of rare plants and insects.

The newcomers brought in their canoes the plants and animals which had been essential in their former homes. Taro, the large leafed plant from which *poi* is made, sugar cane, coconuts, breadfruit, a variety of yam, mountain apples, bamboo, sweet potatoes and gourds were all planted in the soil of this new land. None of these plants were known in Hawaii before the Polynesians arrived. Chickens, dogs and pigs were also brought as food and a type of rat came along as a stowaway.

What the Hawaiians brought

The high chiefs among the Hawaiians were descendants of gods and they ruled their people with absolute authority. When a high chief walked by, commoners prostrated themselves. It was *kapu,* or forbidden, to allow your shadow to fall on the house, or much less, the person of a high chief. Violating these *kapus* brought instant death by war club or strangling.

The kapu system

It was *kapu* for men to eat with women. It was *kapu* for women to eat pork, bananas, coconuts, turtle meat and certain kinds of fish. All the important events in the lives of the people

16

were governed by age-old restrictions. The birth of a child, marriage, building a house or a canoe, and finally death itself required the performance of specified rites. Religious *kahunas,* or priests, conducted the necessary ceremonies.

The chief who could trace his lineage most directly to the gods was king. He might rule an island or part of an island. All lands belonged to him and he appointed lesser chiefs to serve as governors for sections of his kingdom. In return for labor and payment of taxes, commoners could use the land. In time of war, they were expected to serve in the king's army.

The festival time of the year was the *makahiki* season. Then a special god, set atop a high pole, was carried from district to district. Below the god was a cross piece from which billowed sheets of bark cloth, resembling sails. Taxes were collected and the people rested from their labors and enjoyed many different sporting events. Boxing, wrestling, spear throwing, a kind of bowling and foot racing were all popular.

The makahiki season

But the sea was the natural element of the Hawaiians and they excelled at swimming, diving, canoe racing and their national sport of surfing. Great crowds of people cheered their favorites at surfing matches, where champions raced each other toward the shore on fifteen-foot long boards of solid koa wood which might weigh one hundred and sixty pounds. Betting was common on these occasions. A man's total possessions, including his wife and his personal freedom, might ride on the outcome of one race.

The ancient Hawaiians had no written language until the first missionaries composed one for them. In ancient times legends, stories of the gods and the genealogies of chiefs were memorized by persons who showed special ability and this literature was passed from one generation to another. The petroglyphs which the Hawaiians carved on smooth rocks are considered by some to be the beginning of a written language.

Waves near Laie, east coast of Oahu

Lava rock coastline near Koko crater, east shore of Oahu

Lava rock and surf, Hookena, west coast of Hawaii

The isolation of Hawaii was at long last broken when Captain James Cook chanced on the islands in the year 1778. He was sailing from the Society Islands toward the northwest coast of America when the island of Oahu was sighted. Not long afterward the island of Kauai was seen and off the village of Waimea, Cook anchored the RESOLUTION and DISCOVERY. The sight of these two "floating forests" caused great excitement among the Hawaiians.

Captain Cook named the newly discovered island chain the Sandwich Islands in honor of the Earl of Sandwich, then first lord of the admiralty. A brisk trade soon took place between the English and the natives. Hogs, sweet potatoes and fresh water were exchanged for nails and pieces of iron. When a Hawaiian tried to make off with a boat hook from a rowboat which had been pulled up on the beach, he was shot by an English lieutenant. It was the first display of the mighty weapons of the newcomers and the first of many tragedies which Western men would bring to the Hawaiians.

After spending some two weeks at Kauai and the small neighboring island of Niihau, Cook set off for the Pacific northwest. Eight months later, in November of 1778, he returned, hoping to find a protected harbor where he could repair and provision his ships for a trip to the Arctic. He searched the southern coast of Maui and then sailed on to the island of Hawaii where the bay of Kealakekua seemed to well suit his needs.

Captain Cook wrote that a thousand canoes surrounded his ships as they anchored at Kealakekua. Other Hawaiians paddled out on surfboards or simply swam toward the two ships. When they realized the English were going to stay, the natives showed their joy by singing and shouting. The sails of the big ships reminded the Hawaiians of the billowing cloth sheets of the *makahiki* god and so Cook was treated as a god. When he went ashore, priests escorted him to a high temple built above the stony seashore and chanted religious songs in his honor.

In two and a half weeks time, provisions had been stowed aboard, necessary repairs had been made, and the Englishmen departed. But fate would not allow so simple a parting. The two ships ran into a storm off Kohala, the northern tip of Hawaii, and the foremast of the RESOLUTION was severely damaged. Cook ordered a return to Kealakekua Bay for repairs. Once at anchor, the English were again hard put to keep the Hawaiians from stealing everything that could be carried off. One night the DISCOVERY's large cutter was stolen and the next morning, Cook went ashore to persuade the Hawaiian king to come aboard his ship as assurance that the cutter would be returned.

Death of Captain Cook

At first the king was willing, but his chiefs and wives pleaded with him not to go. Cook started toward his long boat, but at the water's edge, he was struck with a club and then stabbed in the back with a dagger. Four of the nine marines who were with him were also killed.

Native huts were burned and some Hawaiians killed during the next several days. Then a sort of truce was managed and some of the bones of Captain James Cook were given up by the Hawaiians. The king placed a *kapu* on the bay and at sunset English flags were flown at half mast. Sailors in blue and white uniforms and marines in red uniforms lined the deck while Captain Clerke read the burial service over the flag draped coffin. The remains of the great captain were lowered into the bay as a ten-gun salute was fired.

For seven years Hawaii lay untouched by foreigners. Then four ships arrived in a single year and after that the Sandwich Islands became popular as a place for ships' crews to rest and a place to obtain fresh meat, vegetables, salt and water. Ships' captains also discovered that the islands were a place where sturdy Hawaiians could be recruited to man whalers and merchantmen.

22

Plaque commemorating Captain Cook's death at Kealakekua Bay, Hawaii

"NEAR THIS SPOT
CAPT. JAMES COOK
WAS KILLED
FEBRUARY 14, 1779
ORIGINAL TABLET DEDICATED
AUGUST 15, 1928 BY
COOK SESQUICENTENNIAL
COMMISSION

As Captain Cook had sailed along the coast of western Maui seeking a suitable port in which to repair his ships he was visited one day by the king of the island of Hawaii who came aboard accompanied by a young chief named Kamehameha. The young chief was destined to become Hawaii's most famous ruler.

Kamehameha was an ambitious, intelligent warrior who realized that the weapons of the Westerners could help him increase his power. While other chiefs freely presented gifts to the English, Kamehameha shrewdly traded his royal cloak of red feathers for a number of specially forged iron daggers. The guns and warlike skills of the newcomers would never be forgotten by the young chief.

After the death of the king of the island of Hawaii, Kamehameha began his plan for the conquest of all the islands. He was a brave, inspirational leader and before long the whole island of Hawaii was under his rule. Among his advisors were two English sailors, John Young and Isaac Davis. Kamehameha had first held them captive, but he won their confidence and eventually made them chiefs. Both men lived out their lives in the service of the Hawaiian kingdom.

*Uniting the
islands*

Kamehameha rigged his double-hulled canoes with Western style sails, mounted cannons on the platforms which bridged the hulls and conquered the islands of Maui, Molokai and Lanai. After a fierce battle on Oahu, where his soldiers drove enemy warriors over the *pali,* or cliffs, of Nuuanu Valley, Kamehameha was in possession of all inhabited islands except Kauai and Niihau. Kamehameha never landed on these islands, but he was accepted there as supreme ruler.

The king constantly traded with ships' captains for supplies of rifles, cannons and ammunition. Although he could neither read nor write, the king was always the master in dealing with foreigners. He was one of the great leaders in the world of the early nineteenth century.

Remains of an ancient highway, built by Kamehameha I, south Kona, Hawaii

Steam vents in Kilauea Crater, Hawaii National Park, Hawaii

Kamehameha demonstrated his decisiveness and power when visiting Russians built a block house and raised their flag at Honolulu. The king immediately dispatched a chief to expel the Russians from Oahu. When the Russians retreated to Kauai, Kamehameha was still not satisfied. He pressured the king of Kauai to force the Russians completely from the islands.

Mourning the death of Kamehameha

Kamehameha's death in 1819 was mourned throughout Hawaii. Captain Otto Von Kotzebue, a German in the service of the Russian navy, anchored his ships in Honolulu harbor in 1824. He visited Queen Nomahanna, one of the late king's wives, and with great emotion the portly Hawaiian lady bared her arm and showed Von Kotzebue an inscription tattooed in Hawaiian. The words read, "Our good King Kamehameha died on the 8th of May, 1819." Many others carried similar inscriptions as a reminder of their king. The anniversary of his death was a day of mourning.

Breaking with the ancient ways

Kamehameha believed in the ancient gods and customs of his ancestors. But even during his lifetime, others began to doubt. Foreigners often broke the old *kapus* and they suffered no harm. Some Hawaiians found they also suffered no harm if they secretly ignored the *kapus*. Faith in the old gods was slowly disappearing.

When Kamehameha's son, Liholiho, became king, he openly broke with the past by sitting down and eating with women at a *luau*. By breaking the eating *kapu*, the new king in one stroke destroyed the foundations of the ancient religion. And because religion was the basis of the whole Hawaiian social system, this social system was destined to also crumble.

A Kiawe tree growing amidst the ruins of an old Russian fort, Waimea, Kauai

Waioli Mission house, Hanalei, Kauai

At the same time that the old ways were being destroyed, a company of missionaries was setting out from New England, bound for Hawaii. When they arrived in Hawaii in 1820, garbed in frock coats and ankle length dresses, they found a religious vacuum which they tried to fill by converting the Hawaiians to Christianity.

The coming of the missionaries

King Liholiho granted the missionaries the right to establish stations at Kailua on Hawaii and at Honolulu for a trial period of one year. The instructions which the missionaries carried with them said they were to spread the Word of God by preaching, teaching and printing.

The missionaries had been moved to come to Hawaii by tales of sailors who had visited the islands and by the widely circulated story of Henry Obookiah, a young Hawaiian who had traveled to New England and lamented the fact that his people lived in spiritual darkness. The energetic missionaries worked without rest. Once they had been given permission to stay a year, they were never to leave.

Now began one of the greatest literacy movements ever recorded. In less than two years time, the missionaries had composed a written Hawaiian language and had begun to print reading and spelling books. More missionaries came from New England to join the first company and many Hawaiians were trained to teach in the schools. In 1832 some 52,000 students, many of them adults, sat as students in some 1,100 grass thatched school buildings. Churches likewise had been established throughout all the islands.

Founding schools and churches

The missionaries at once were at odds with many of the sea captains who frequented Hawaiian ports. These captains often exploited the Hawaiians without mercy. They induced the chiefs to strip the mountains of fragrant sandalwood trees and traded guns, fancy clothing, gin and even dilapidated sailing ships for this wood which they then sold in China. When the

31

Hawaiians could not cut enough sandalwood to meet the demands of the traders, the chiefs were given goods on credit, causing them to fall hopelessly into debt.

King Liholiho saw only the beginning of this battle between missionaries and traders. In 1823 he sailed from Honolulu with his favorite wife for England. Liholiho wanted to gain advice on governing his kingdom and perhaps he even wished to place the Hawaiian Islands under the protection of George IV. Liholiho and his queen reached London, but there they were stricken with measles and died before they had an audience with the king. Their bodies were returned to Hawaii on board a British warship under the command of Lord Byron, a cousin of the famous poet.

Conflict between missionaries and sailors

The kingdom now passed to the late king's younger brother, who became known as Kamehameha III. The new ruler was a ten-year-old boy at the time of Liholiho's death, so Kaahumanu, favorite wife of Kamehameha I, acted as a regent until the new king came of age.

A boy king

These were puzzling years for Hawaii's rulers. Born in the security of ancient ways, they now suddenly faced the problems of the nineteenth century western world. Many foreigners, particularly Americans, were settling in the islands. Sailors crowded the port towns of Lahaina and Honolulu. To control the situation, the chiefs, with counsel from the missionaries, made their first attempt at passing laws. When a law was agreed upon, criers proclaimed these laws to the people. Among the laws passed was one requiring proper observance of the Sabbath. The chiefs also seriously considered making the Ten Commandments the law of the land. Laws restricting liquor and the free access of women on board ships were resented by many sailors.

In 1826 the conflict between missionary-inspired laws and the desires of many sailors exploded when the U.S.S. DOLPHIN

32

dropped anchor in Honolulu harbor. Lieutenant Percival, in command of the warship, demanded that women be allowed aboard his ship, a custom which had made the islands popular throughout the Pacific. In an interview with Queen Kaahumanu, Percival was refused and he placed the blame on Rev. Hiram Bingham, Honolulu's most influential missionary. When threats failed, Percival turned his sailors loose. On a Sunday afternoon, gangs of seamen roamed the dusty streets of Honolulu. They smashed the windows of the royal residence of Queen Kaahumanu and surrounded Bingham at the door of his house. Bingham's life was possibly saved by club swinging Hawaiians who battled to his rescue. Once in the fray the Hawaiians seemed to enjoy the fight and Bingham had to restrain them from beating out the brains of fallen sailors, a custom their fathers had practiced only a few years earlier.

Violence between missionaries and sailors

In desperation Governor Boki, a member of the ruling council with Kaahumanu, gave in to the demands of Percival and ordered the *kapu* raised, allowing boat loads of women to board the DOLPHIN. It was a bitter, disillusioning lesson for both the missionaries and the chiefs. The U.S.S. DOLPHIN was the first American man-of-war to visit Hawaii. By contrast Lord Byron, who had recently sailed from the islands, had behaved ideally. For many years to come the rulers of Hawaii would strongly favor the English over the Americans.

By 1840 the Catholics also had established a mission in Honolulu and began their efforts to convert the Hawaiians. They too had brought a printing press, which continued to operate for some fifty years. In the early years the Catholics were opposed by both the Protestant missionaries and the Hawaiian chiefs. Their presence was reinforced, however, by the appearance of French warships from time to time and eventually they were accepted.

Arrival of Catholic missionaries

France and Great Britain annexed a number of island groups in the Pacific in the early 1840's and fears that Hawaii might be included proved well founded when Britisher Lord George Paulet arrived in Honolulu harbor aboard the CARYSFORT early in 1843. Lord Paulet made demands on the king which were impossible to meet and on February 25 the Hawaiian flag was lowered and the British flag raised.

Five months later Rear Admiral Thomas of the British navy arrived in Honolulu to right the wrong done by Paulet. The Hawaiian flag was again raised and Kamehameha III was given a twenty-one gun salute to show that he was the sovereign of the Hawaiian Islands.

Since the 1820's business in Hawaii centered around the whale-ships which stopped at Lahaina and Honolulu. Between 1843 and 1854 an average of 419 ships anchored at these ports annually. Large quantities of food were purchased, ship repairs of all kinds were required and thousands of sailors spent many months' pay in town.

Whalers were a source of income for Hawaii, but they brought many problems. Mountains were stripped of trees and hundreds of derelict seamen were put ashore to fend for themselves. Ships' captains also recruited Hawaiians as seamen and up to one-fifth of the young men of Hawaii were sailing the seas during the whaling era. This was one reason for the rapid decline in island population during these years.

Some businessmen realized that whaling ships would eventually have to find other oceans in which to hunt their prizes or perhaps other ports in the Pacific would become more convenient supply bases. These businessmen wished to find a more stable economic base. Raising cattle, tobacco and coffee were tried, but the most successful venture was sugar. In the year 1836 four tons of sugar were exported. By 1850 plantations had been established on all the major islands and exports had risen to 375 tons.

Sunrise, Hilo harbor, east coast of Hawaii

The opening of the Oregon territory and the discovery of gold in California had a profound effect on Hawaii. In 1848 hundreds of island people, both Hawaiians and foreigners, rushed to the gold fields. At the same time island stores and warehouses were stripped of all goods which could be used in California. In winter time some miners came to Hawaii, returning to the gold fields when the mountain snows had melted. During these chaotic years prices of goods fluctuated just as wildly in the islands as in California.

From the gold rush days on, trade with California largely replaced trade with Atlantic coast ports. Hawaii was now tied by its first strong economic bond to the United States.

When Kamehameha III died in 1854 his nephew, Liholiho, was crowned Kamehameha IV. The new king was a bright young man of twenty-one. He had traveled in England and had developed a strong preference for English ways. Kamehameha IV married the granddaughter of the Englishman John Young. At the request of the royal couple the English Episcopal Church came to Hawaii. Weakened by a life-long struggle with asthma and by grief over the death of his only son, the king died at the age of twenty-nine.

Liholiho's elder brother, Prince Lot, now came to the throne as Kamehameha V. The new king was a stout man with curly black hair and long sideburns. In affairs of state he was a stubborn but practical man who worked to obtain recognition of Hawaiian independence from the United States and from European countries. During his nine years of rule he wrote a constitution giving strong powers to the king and limiting the right to vote to those who could read and write and who held property. He died in 1872 without leaving an heir or naming a successor to the throne of Hawaii.

For the first time the people of Hawaii could express their preference for a king by voting in a plebiscite. The ballot count was heavily in favor of handsome, personable William Lunalilo over David Kalakaua. The legislature confirmed Lunalilo by unanimously naming him king, but just thirteen months after his election the new king was dead, a victim of tuberculosis.

These were years of dramatic change. The fact that the *haoles,* or foreigners, were steadily gaining in power was clearly shown by the late King Lunalilo's cabinet, which did not include one Hawaiian. The Hawaiian population continued to decrease at a terrifying rate. Principally because of disease, the number of people in the islands dropped to less than 60,000 in 1872. A conservative estimate in Captain James Cook's day, just ninety-four years earlier, was a population of 300,000 people.

Whaling activity in the Pacific was slowing down. Petroleum had been discovered in Pennsylvania in 1859 and this eventually took the place of whale oil. During the American Civil

Grave marker and Banyan tree roots, Honolulu, Oahu

Herding cattle on the Parker Ranch, near Kamuela, Hawaii

War many whalers had been sunk, but the death blow was administered in 1871 when thirty whalers were lost during an early freeze in the Arctic. Sugar growing was now looked to as the economic salvation of the islands.

In April 1875 a reciprocity treaty was at last signed with the United States. This meant that sugar could enter the United States duty free and U.S. produced goods received the same privilege in the islands. An agricultural boom immediately followed in Hawaii. During the next ten years sugar tonnage increased ten times over. Although public sentiment favored British influence over American, economic reality had now clearly linked Hawaii's destiny with that of the United States.

David Kalakaua again campaigned for the throne after the passing of Lunalilo. He was opposed by Queen Dowager Emma, widow of Kamehameha IV. When the legislature elected Kalakaua king in 1874 the courthouse in which the legislature met was attacked by a mob of the Queen's supporters and many members were beaten. It was the beginning of a hazardous, hectic reign for the new king.

Kalakaua was a well educated, witty man who was called the "Merry Monarch" by his subjects. He surrounded himself with questionable advisors, however, and squandered great sums of money on royal trappings which the little kingdom could ill afford. He embarked on a grand round-the-world tour, and while in Japan proposed a royal marriage which would unite the two nations. He built Iolani Palace and tried to unite islands in southern Polynesia with Hawaii to form a Polynesian kingdom, with himself as emperor.

During his reign most *haoles* gradually lost confidence in the monarchy. In 1891 after seventeen years as king, Kalakaua died while visiting San Francisco. For all practical purposes the monarchy was dead too, because sugar planters and other businessmen could no longer tolerate the turmoil of the kingdom. They looked to the United States for a new stability.

Sugar mill and ship near Hilo, east coast of Hawaii

*Liliuokalani
becomes
queen*

Liliuokalani, the sister of Kalakaua, now assumed the throne. She was an imposing woman, fifty-one years of age and resolute as granite. Her wishes were to restore the old Hawaiian system and rumors of the day said she even wanted to disenfranchise all foreigners.

Revolution

By 1893 a group of annexationists decided on a desperate move. Under the leadership of tall, white bearded Judge Sanford Ballard Dole they took action. A force of men took over the government buildings in an uprising which, surprisingly, saw only one man wounded. The success of the revolution seemed confirmed when marines were landed from the United States cruiser, BOSTON, to protect American property.

Although a counter-revolution attempt was made, the Provisional Government was never in danger. For a while Liliuokalani hoped the annexationists would not be recognized in Washington, D. C., but she was disappointed and there was little she could do. The Hawaiian monarchy was now only a memory.

*Palm frond on the
lava rock shore at the
City of Refuge near
Honaunau, Hawaii*

Some wise Hawaiians had seen annexation coming fifty years before it occurred and they had pleaded with their king to send the foreigners away. The American-led revolts which had overthrown Mexican rule in California and Texas added to their apprehensions. But after Kamehameha I the Hawaiian rulers were not strong enough to rally their people against the modern forces they faced. It might, indeed, have been impossible for any ruler to have stemmed the tide of foreign domination.

The revolutionists were mostly Americans, many of whom had been born in the islands and were Hawaiian citizens. They were a determined and aggressive group. For many years to come they would remain the leaders of Hawaii.

Even before the revolution Hawaii was changing in many ways. Improved shipping lines were established between the various islands and between Hawaii and the mainland. Roads and bridges were constructed and railroads carried passengers and freight on Maui, Hawaii and Oahu. One of the first banks west of the Rocky Mountains was established in Honolulu in 1858 and the first telephone lines were strung on Maui in 1878.

Economic growth

Many problems bothered the early sugar growers, but perhaps the most nagging was the scarcity of labor. Because of the tragic decline in Hawaii's population there were not enough hands to work the fields. Without an adequate labor supply, sugar had no future.

At first it was hoped Polynesians from other Pacific islands could be recruited and brought to Hawaii to work on the plantations. This plan, however, was unsuccessful. Only a few immigrants came and most of these returned to their homes after serving out their contracts.

More immigrants

In 1852 three hundred Chinese came to Hawaii under five year contracts. By 1866 their number had grown to 1,300. Most of the newcomers were single men. Many married Hawaiian women and remained in the islands. Other races also came. A prominent Islander, Dr. William Hillebrand, suggested that

Portuguese from the Madeira Islands would fit in well in Hawaii. Subsequently, arrangements were made and the first shipload of Portuguese arrived in Hawaii.

An increased population

The largest group of newcomers were the Japanese. The first small band of workers came as early as 1868. Not until 1885, however, did large groups arrive. Some women came, but single men often secured "picture brides" by selecting a future wife from Japan on the basis of photographs. In the two years between 1898 and the turn of the century some 30,000 Japanese came. By then Hawaii's total population was 154,000, two-fifths of whom were Japanese.

Many other races came to join Hawaii's cosmopolitan population. In 1903 the first Koreans came and three years later the first Filipino families arrived. Joining them were more immigrants from nearly every country in Europe and also from the United States.

The original idea in importing labor was to bring in young, single men who would devote a number of years to plantation work and then return to their homelands. After 1890, however, more and more workers decided to remain in Hawaii after their contracts had been completed.

Labor unions

Hawaii's labor unions, particularly on the plantations, can trace their beginnings from this era. Several large scale strikes took place on sugar plantations in the early 1900's. Feelings ran high and sometimes the result was violence. Labor, however, had little real power. Unions were organized mostly along racial lines and what little unity there was, lasted only during strike periods.

After World War II the labor union movement in Hawaii gained quickly. Sugar and pineapple workers, longshoremen, state and county workers organized strong unions. Their influence is now felt at the bargaining table and also at the polls.

As a Territory, Hawaii became a more stable community. The economy of the islands moved ahead as sugar proved to

Old Japanese headstone, near Olowalu, west coast of Maui

be a steady source of income year after year. After the turn of the century James D. Dole, a distant relative of Judge Dole, harvested his first pineapple crop. Pineapples could be grown on upland plains, land not ideally suited to sugar cane, so there was no conflict between the two crops. Soon pineapple was a source of income second only to sugar.

Pineapple

Ships arrived more frequently to carry Hawaii's sugar and pineapple to mainland markets and return with the variety of merchandise needed in the islands. On these ships came the first flow of tourists who found the beach at Waikiki very much to their liking.

Tourism

The first successful air flight to Honolulu was made in June 1927 when Army lieutenants Lester Maitland and Albert Hegenberger flew from Oakland, California, to Oahu in less than twenty-six hours. Only eight years after this, in 1935, the Pan American China Clipper began service between California and the Orient, stopping over at Honolulu.

Hawaii made rapid strides toward becoming a modern American community during the first three decades of the twentieth century. In Honolulu old frame buildings gave way to modern concrete structures. Homes were built in the valleys and up the hillsides behind Honolulu. Pearl Harbor became an important base for the U. S. Pacific fleet. The Army built Schofield Barracks, on the cool upland plateau of Oahu, and Hickam Field, near Pearl Harbor, provided a runway for Air Force planes.

During these three decades more and more plantation workers moved to Honolulu after fulfilling their labor contracts. Many of them began their own businesses. By choosing to remain in Hawaii, a certain tie with the lands of their birth had been broken. Their children were now educated in island schools and the ambitions of the second generation became typically American.

Growth of Honolulu

On December 7, 1941, the course of Hawaii's history changed. On that fateful Sunday Japanese warplanes attacked the military bases on Oahu and the name, Hawaii, became known in every household across the United States. Men and women who six months earlier had never heard of Pearl Harbor were soon sailing into this port as soldiers, sailors and marines. For a time Hawaii was the front line of defense in the Pacific.

World War II

In the days following the Japanese attack, islanders lived in fear of enemy air raids or invasion. Freighters were sunk within sight of the islands by enemy submarines. Submarines also shelled installations on Hawaii, Maui and Kauai. Tension reached a peak in May 1942 when rumors spread that the Japanese were planning to invade the islands.

Battle of Midway

The rumors seemed based on fact when downtown Honolulu was ordered evacuated. All military leaves were cancelled, temporary hospital facilities were readied and civilian businessmen, called Defense Volunteers, were called to duty. Finally on June 4 a Navy communique said Midway Island was under attack. The streets of Honolulu were nearly deserted. A Japanese invasion was expected.

Then on June 6 came the cheering news of the famous naval victory at Midway. The fear of invasion had at last been removed. Later the battle of Midway would be known as the turning point of the war in the Pacific.

At first some were skeptical of the patriotism of Hawaii's new, mixed population. But the war records compiled by island men and women were too impressive to permit skepticism. Most publicized was Hawaii's 442nd Regimental Combat Team, made up of Japanese-Americans. Two weeks after returning from some of the bloodiest fighting in Europe, the 442nd paraded in Washington, D.C. and President Truman stood in a drenching rain to tie the Presidential Distinguished

War record

Unit Citation banners to the colors of the unit.

At war's end Hawaii entered a new era. Islanders were able
to attend the finest mainland universities through the G. I. Bill

*A new
confidence*

of Rights. These people quickly assumed positions of leadership in business, the professions and in politics. World War II
had brought a new sense of confidence to Hawaii's citizens.

Hawaii's fight for statehood goes back as far as 1903 when

Statehood

the Territorial legislature petitioned Congress for admission
as a state. In 1919 Delegate to Congress Kalanianaole intro-
duced in Congress the first of many bills to grant statehood to
Hawaii. Succeeding delegates worked to overcome indifference
and a lack of knowledge in Congress concerning the island
community of Hawaii.

At long last, in March 1959 both houses of Congress passed
by overwhelming majorities a bill to grant statehood to Hawaii.
A state plebiscite was held and Hawaii's citizens voted for Statehood seventeen to one. In July an election was held in the
islands. The results showed what a unique democracy Hawaii
really was. The appointed Territorial governor, William F.
Quinn, born in New York state, was elected governor. Oren E.
Long, a Kansas-born educator, was elected U. S. Senator along
with Hiram Fong, a Chinese-American. Daniel K. Inouye, a
Japanese-American war hero, was elected to the U. S. House
of Representatives.

The opportunity to play an international role was given

*East-West
Center*

Hawaii in 1959 when Delegate to Congress, John A. Burns,
announced that Congress had appropriated money for the
establishment of an East-West Center on the campus of the
University of Hawaii. For the first time scholarship funds allow
a large number of men and women of different cultures, re-
ligions and races to learn about, and respect each other.

Chiefs, kings, sailors, missionaries, laborers, soldiers, mer-
chants—men and women from nearly every part of the world

48

have helped to weave the pattern of Hawaiian history. In two centuries time these peoples of diverse cultures have gathered within the confines of an island group and have lived in tolerance and understanding of each other. This, perhaps, is Hawaii's unique contribution to the twentieth century.

Hawaii's contribution

EDWARD JOESTING

Clouds in the sky over Molokai

Mauna Kea, left, and Mauna Loa on the island of Hawaii as seen across Alenuihaha Channel from Haleakala, Maui

The late Naluahine Kaopua, resident of the Kona coast, west Hawaii

A recent lava flow which is still steaming,
Puna district, east coast of Hawaii

Hanakapiai, along the north shore of Kauai

Kamehameha V coconut grove, near Kaunakakai,
south coast of Molokai

Kalalau Valley, northwest coast of Kauai

Tidal pool in the crevice of an ancient lava flow, near Honaunau, Hawaii

Na Pali coastline from Haena, Kauai

60

*Parker Ranch cowboys, near Kamuela,
island of Hawaii* *

*Photograph by Virginia Adams

*Saint Joseph's Church, built by Father Damien
Kamalo, Molokai* *

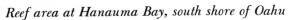

Reef area at Hanauma Bay, south shore of Oahu

Small island off Laniloa Point, Laie, Oahu

Hanalei Bay, north shore of Kauai

NEXT PAGE: *The Pali lookout and a section of the Koolau Range, Oahu* →

Blooming Primavera tree, Honolulu, Oahu

*Leaves of a variety of Caladium,
Foster Botanical Garden, Oahu*

Coastline near Waialua, Oahu

*Sugar cane field
and mountains
near Lahaina, Maui*

Mauna Kea from the slopes of Mauna Loa, on the island of Hawaii

Coastline near Kalapana, on the east shore of Hawaii

Wainiha Bay, north shore of the island of Kauai

No alien land in all the world has any deep strong charm
for me but that one, no other land could so longingly
and so beseechingly haunt me, sleeping and waking,
through half a lifetime, as that one has done.
Other things leave me, but it abides; other things change,
but it remains the same. For me its balmy airs are
always blowing, its summer seas flashing in the sun;
the pulsing of its surfbeat is in my ear; I can see
its garlanded crags, its leaping cascades, its plumy palms
drowsing by the shore, its remote summits floating
like islands above the cloud rack; I can feel the spirit
of its woodland solitudes, I can hear the plash
of its brooks; in my nostrils still lives the breath of flowers
that perished twenty years ago.

MARK TWAIN

Moon over Koko Head, south coast of Oahu

Cinder cone in the crater of Haleakala, Maui

Rain forest, near Kilauea crater,
Hawaii National Park, Hawaii

Ferns and Norfolk Island Pine trees, near Mt. Lanaihale, Lanai

*Makapuu Point, east coast of **Oahu***

"HILO 35 M," *an old mileage marker, near Kalapana,*
east coast of Hawaii

Fish pond at dawn, near Kaunakakai,
south coast of Molokai

OVER:

Waves off the eastern shore of Oahu

Detail of an ancient Hawaiian wall at the City of Refuge,
near Honaunau, west coast of Hawaii

Windows of an abandoned church
near South Point, south Hawaii

Fern and old church at Keanae, north coast of Maui

Along the road near Haena, north shore of Kauai

Cemetery beside Sodo Mission, Mantokuji Temple, Paia, Maui

Church at sunrise, Waiohinu, south Hawaii

A lava blister in Mauna Loa Game and Forest Reserve, central Hawaii

Roots of a Banyan tree, Foster Botanical Garden, Honolulu, Oahu

83

Evening clouds over the West Maui mountains, above Wailuki, Maui

Rain clouds over sugar cane fields, central plain of Maui

Hawaiian Koa tree, in the Bird Park,
Hawaii Volcanoes National Park, Hawaii

Metamorphosed lava detail,
near Honokohau,
north shore of Maui

Church, Halawa Valley, east shore of Molokai

Silver Sword plant, in the crater of Haleakala, Maui

*Pineapple fields
near Wahiawa,
central Oahu*

90

PHOTOGRAPHY IN THE HAWAIIAN ISLANDS

The purpose of this article is to assist the photographer to master some of the problems he will encounter in the Hawaiian Islands. No place on earth is more enticing to both the serious photographer and the snapshooter. The professional also comes under the spell, but soon recognizes the basic problems and may proceed with more caution than does the enthusiastic visitor of amateur status. To capture the magical beauty of the Islands requires sensitivity, technique and patience.

The qualities which are favorable to color photography—soft landscape colors accented by bright flowers, costumes and sunsets—present some special problems with black-and-white photography. The values and colors of lush vegetation, lava rock and sky have a tendency to merge and the usual soft atmospheric effects further reduce the contrast of the landscape (except at high altitudes). On the other hand, the contrast of near objects—foliage, rocks, architecture and people—is about normal.

With a few exceptions the Hawaiian scene is dominated by the ocean horizon, the long slopes of the great volcanoes, and the intricate jumble of lush vegetation. The shorelines of dark lava and white surf challenge any kind of photography. Certain bold features, such as the Napali Coast, the jagged splendor of the Pali and the cliffs and cinder cones of Haleakala, are as dramatic and awe-inspiring as any scenic displays of their kind in the world. Of course, the infinitude of small details of nature on land and by (as well as in) the sea are rewarding to the photographer equipped to handle them. The evidence of pre-history and the historic culture of the Islands, the remnants of the pure native population, and the beauty of the present complex racial types offer many exciting opportunities for interpretative and creative photography.

We must think about the limitations of our mediums (black-and-white or color) in reference to the qualities of the subjects and the conditions of atmosphere and illumination. Pre-visualization of the desired picture is essential. Few special techniques are indicated, but the selection of the standard techniques will require some thought and experimentation. Space does not allow for an adequate description of the Zone System approach but sources are listed in the Bibliography on Page 98. Photographs, black-and-white or in color, cannot *duplicate* reality; they can only *simulate* certain aspects of reality. What is *real* to one person may be quite *unreal* to another. We can accept the pictorial symbols of value, texture, form and color, and we can enjoy the photograph as an esthetic object without reference to the "realities" of the subject. Every photographer has the privilege of seeing the world in his own way and expressing it in terms of his own imagination.

Special fields of work, such as aerial and underwater photography, are adequately covered in the literature of photography. Reference is made here to *Photographic Literature*, edited by Albert Boni, New York, Morgan and Morgan, 1962. It contains a tremendous number of references to works on practically every application of photography as well as its history and techniques.

EQUIPMENT

Selection of cameras, lenses and accessories is in few ways different from the usual. However, the *protection* of equipment and materials from the effects of heat-plus-humidity is very important. Hawaii is only semitropical but the combination of temperatures up to 95° with a relative humidity of 85% can be debilitating to the photographer and harmful to his films and equipment. The photographer can acclimatize and dress (or undress) for comfort, but his apparatus and materials will need attention and protection.

Camera and film left standing in ordinary cases in the sun for any length of time will suffer from heat-plus-humidity. All cases should be painted brilliant white; this will reflect most of the sun's heat and keep the contents relatively cool. Do not expose cameras (when out of their cases) for long in the direct sun; they will absorb heat and perhaps damage the film within them. Cameras carried about on tripods or neck-straps can be protected by enclosing them in white plastic bags. At home store them in as dry and cool a place as possible. Before putting away be sure all dampness is carefully wiped off all parts of the cameras, shutters, lenses, film-holders, etc. Lenses should be carefully cleaned with proper lens-cleaning fluid and tissues. In shore areas, subject to salty surf spray, it is especially important that cameras and lenses be most carefully wiped off and dried before replacing in cases. If stored for any length of time under damp conditions mold or fungus growths may appear—even on the surface of lenses! The use of desiccants such as silica-gel during storage periods is strongly advised.

Conditions vary in different parts of the Islands; in the Rain Forests humidity can be extremely high but in the southern and western areas rather arid conditions may prevail, such as at the Kona District and along the western slopes of Oahu. Areas such as those around Hilo and Honolulu have moderate heat and humidity. At high elevations (Mauna Loa, Haleakala, etc.) freezing conditions are sometimes encountered.

MATERIALS

All standard films—conventional and Polaroid Land films—together with Ciné film of all kinds, can be used with success. A basic rule—store all materials under dry and cool conditions, protect while in use, and process as soon as possible after exposure. Always store developed negatives in separate envelopes, protecting them with a fold of non-hygroscopic material such as Glassene paper. Obviously, laboratory procedures must be adjusted to temperature of darkroom, solutions and tap water.

USEFUL ACCESSORIES

VIEWING FILTER (Wratten #90). Obtainable in 2", 3" and 4" gels and in "B" Glass. A valuable aid to visualization of the subject in terms of black-and-white rendition. Colors of different hue but of similar value may merge as similar values in black-and-white; the Wratten #90 viewing filter transforms the scene into near-monochrome values, and clearly shows what areas of the subject will merge in value, or show as different values, on un-filtered panchromatic film. By inference it will suggest what color filter should be used to obtain optimum separation of subject values. For example, average foliage and gray rock—quite different in *color*—might be rendered as the same value of gray with un-filtered panchromatic film. A blue or red filter would render the foliage *darker* than the rock; a strong green filter would render it *lighter* than the rock. The #90 filter is for *viewing* only—it must not be used over the lens when taking the picture. Obviously it has no value in color photography.

STANDARD COLOR FILTERS. The most efficient filter for general landscape work in Hawaii is the Wratten #12 (minus-blue) filter. It falls between the #8 (K2) and the #15 (G). An exposure factor of 2x is appropriate except for very clear days and at high altitudes where, with a greater proportion of blue in the light, the factor might be 3x and even higher. As we move towards the practical limits of the "contrast" filter series we have (all filters available in glass or cut gelatine sheets):

FILTER	FACTOR	REMARKS
#15.G (orange)	about 3x	Rejects all blue, slightly darkens green, lightens orange and red.
#23.E (light red)	4x	Rejects blue and most green light. Favors red.
#25.A (red)	8x	Rejects blue and green. Transmits red.
#29.F (dark red)	12-15x	Rejects all but deep red light and gives maximum contrast in landscape and cloud pictures.

A fern detail in the Rain forest, near Kilauea crater, Hawaii National Park, Hawaii

The E filter is recommended for distant landscapes; almost as effective as the A filter, it requires only 4x instead of 8x exposure factor. The B (#58) is a strong green filter; exposure factor about 8x. It transmits green and rejects blue and red light. It is very useful with foliage. The C⁵ (#47) is a strong blue filter; exposure factor about 6x. It transmits blue light and rejects green and red light. It gives a lighter rendition of shadows illuminated from the blue sky and therefore "softens" harshly illuminated subjects. It renders the blue sky very light in value. With the C filter and panchromatic film we obtain effects quite similar to those with the old "color-blind" emulsions.

With panchromatic film the Wratten #38 and #66 (minus-red) filters produce the "orthochromatic" effect, as they transmit only blue and green light. Orthochromatic film is often superior to panchromatic film in the rendition of foliage, skin, etc., but of course skies are lighter and clouds less distinct.

The color values of nature are very complex; there is seldom, if ever, anything in nature which we could call a *pure* color; that is, a color of high saturation. The blue sky reflects varying proportions of green and red light in addition to the dominant blue light; even with a very strong red filter we will not get a completely black sky because of the small amount of red light reflected. The same applies to green foliage; some greens reflect quite a lot of blue light (as well as infra-red). Hence, we sometimes expect stronger filter effects than we obtain, because we are not aware of the diluted quality of most natural colors.

The eye is hyper-sensitive to green and sees foliage somewhat lighter in value than does the un-filtered panchromatic film. Hence, to achieve a realistic balance of values we should "place" the luminance value of the foliage about one zone higher on the exposure scale than its measured luminance would indicate. However, using filters such as the Wratten #11 with panchromatic film, or using orthochromatic film without a filter, the film will react to foliage green about the same as does the eye.

THE POLARIZER. This is the only device which will give dark skies with color photography (when used at about 90° to the sun). It also darkens skies with black-and-white photography and helps reduce haze in distant scenes. It permits removal of unwanted reflections, wholly or in part, when directed to the subject at an angle of about 56°. Polarizers have an exposure factor of about 2.5x or 3x (in reference to the unpolarized areas of the subject). The polarizing effect can be visually appreciated; the polarizer is rotated about its axis until the desired effect is obtained. Then, placed over the lens at this optimum position, the effect is duplicated in the negative. The polarizing effect can be seen on the ground glass of view cameras and in the image in single-lens reflex finders, etc. It should be remembered that removal of too much reflection from naturally reflective surfaces will alter the character of the object photographed. At the proper viewing angle we can remove sky reflections from water surfaces and see clearly into the depths. Reflections from glass, polished wood, glaring roads, etc., can be controlled but specular light reflected from metals cannot be. Color filters can be used with polarizers, achieving rather startling effects of contrast. In combining the polarizer with a color filter, be certain to *multiply* the exposure factors—NOT add them. With 3x exposure factor for the polarizer and 8x factor for the "A" filter, the combined exposure factor would be 24x, not 11x.

EXPOSURE PHOTOMETERS AND EXPOSURE METERS. As discussed in the *Basic Photo* books and in others listed in the Bibliography, the "spot" photometer, when properly used, is superior to any ordinary exposure meter. The S.E.I. Exposure Photometer, and the Heiland 3/21° Exposure Meter are excellent devices; the first is visually read by adjusting the illuminated "spot" to the surrounding field. The second is a fully instrumented device with a sensitive needle indicating light-value numbers. An extremely precise instrument—the A-500 Luminance analyzer (Gamma Scientific, Inc., San Diego, California)—is now available. With these devices very accurate measurements of small areas of the subject can be made from the camera position. They are, of course, designed for serious photographers; nevertheless, they are fairly simple to use.

EXPOSURE METERS are of two basic types: the Incident-Light Meter, such as the Spectra and Norwood, and the Reflected-Light Meter, such as the Weston, General Electric, etc. Many modern cameras are equipped with built-in meters which are linked in various ways to the shutter mechanism—sometimes achieving fully automatic control. The most remarkable device of this last group is the electronic shutter of the new #100 Polaroid Land camera which responds to a tremendous range of illumination and automatically determines exposures from several seconds to 1/1200 second.

My strong preference is for the Weston III and IV meters as they have the most efficient computing dials on which the luminances of the subject can be related to the entire exposure range of the film. The new Weston V meter uses arbitrary numbers instead of the classic candle-per-square-foot units (c/ft²). A table can be made up relating all the numbers to their equivalent c/ft² values. No. 12 of this new number system equals 100 c/ft²; No. 11 equals 50 c/ft²; No. 13 equals 200 c/ft², and so on.

Reflected-light meters, *as commonly used,* read the average luminance of all the subject areas within the field of view of the meter. The specific luminances cannot be known by this averaging method, and optimum exposures are based on experience and judgment as well as on the meter indications. With sufficiently large areas of the subject the Weston meter can be held fairly close and therefore becomes a "photometer" and with far more accurate results than when the average-field method is employed. In many cases a more accurate average reading is obtained when the meter is pointed down, thereby avoiding inclusion of bright sky areas in the field. This does *not* work when the near foreground is white surf or bright beach sand! Protect exposure meters from heat, such as will accumulate in auto glove compartments on sunny days.

WHITE FOCUSING CLOTH. For those who use standard view cameras a focusing cloth lined with black fabric on one side and brilliant white fabric on the other will provide both function and comfort; the white side will protect both the photographer and his equipment from the heat of the sun. The cloth should never be folded away in the camera case if damp with rain or spray!

LENS SHADE. These are advised for all situations, especially when working into the light or in glaring surroundings. Lens shades reduce glare from unwanted light entering the camera through the lens from outside the actual picture area recorded on the film. It is important that the lens shade does not vignette the image (cut into the corners of the picture field). If the shade is too small, or projects too far in front of the lens (perhaps because of added filters), this effect may occur. It may be difficult to see on the ground glass or in the penta-prism finder when the lens is at full aperture; as the lens is stopped down the edges of the lens shade may come a little into focus and darken the corners of the picture. With cameras that have rising and sliding front and back assemblies, and/or tilting front assembly, we must be very careful to check if the lens shade is vignetting the image in other than normal position of the lens. A lens shade that works well with an 80mm lens may seriously vignette the picture if used on a 50mm lens.

TRIPOD. A *firm* tripod is essential for precise work. The *weight* of the tripod obviously relates to the weight of the camera. The slightest movement of the camera during exposure will blur the image—and this may be painfully apparent when big enlargements are made from small negatives or when small color slides are projected. Vibration from wind, shutter operation, jarring of floors, etc., can all have troublesome effect. Check the tripod carefully with the camera you intend to use with it. A tripod may be truly firm, but the *tripod head* subject to vibration.

MINOR ACCESSORIES:

FOCUSING MAGNIFIER (for use with ground-glass view cameras).

LENS BRUSH AND LENS TISSUE. Important to have on hand at all times.

PLASTIC RAIN PROTECTOR. Of obvious value (might combine with focusing cloth).

METAL TAPE (in inches and/or cms.). Valuable with close-up work where lens extensions must be measured and exposure factors calculated.

GEL FILTER ALBUMS. Snapshot albums (plastic leaves) about 4″ square provide good protection for gel filters. Metal filter holders for 2″ and 3″ are available for gel filters.

LEVEL. Important for architectural work and for assuring level horizons.

FLASH EQUIPMENT. Apart from its obvious use as a prime light source, flash can be helpful in supporting low shadow values in near subjects. Usually, when used as a fill-in light, we should employ a guide number about 2x that for regular lighting; use G. No. 200 instead of G. No. 100, for example. This gives *one-fourth* the usual exposure value and, in addition to the existing daylight, will give good shadow values. Flash fill-in light may cast secondary shadows and the flash light should be placed as close to the lens axis as possible.

ACCESSORIES FOR COLOR PHOTOGRAPHY: Color-temperature meter, polarizer, skylight filter, light-balancing filters, such as Kodak series 81 and 82. Tungsten-to-daylight conversion filter. Compensating filters for special work.

EXTRA PARTS: Tripod screws, cable releases, stop-watch, small pair of pliers, small screwdriver, extra lens caps, extra film slides, extra gel filters.

NOTE BOOK. It is most helpful to keep extensive notes of exposures. The Ansel Adams Exposure Record (Morgan and Morgan, New York) is available in two sizes—pocket size and 8¾ x 5⅓ inches. Also, tables relating to filter and lens-extension factors, film speeds, reciprocity effect and true shutter speeds will be very useful. The true speeds of most shutters vary from the listed speeds, and can be determined by modern electronic devices. A complete *check-list* of all equipment is valuable—providing it is used. Leaving essential items at home can be a frustrating experience!

LIGHTING CONDITIONS, SUBJECT VALUES, ETC.

Perhaps our first impression is that Hawaii is a very "bright" place. The south coast of the big island (Hawaii) is approximately on the latitude of Mexico City. Hence, at any time of the year the sun is a little higher in the sky and the shadows a little shorter than in the continental United States. The direct sunlight might be slightly more intense than in more northerly latitudes but the effect of "brightness" is, in my opinion, due to the amount of water vapor in the atmosphere. Because of this the sky is less blue and reflects and scatters more light than in more arid regions and higher elevations. Actually, objects and surfaces in full sunlight reflect about the same amount of light they would in California; the shadows are softer—that is, their luminances are relatively higher than would be the case under deep blue skies. Conditions of rain, mist, fog, etc., are about the same as anywhere else. Water vapor in the open sky might not be apparent to the eye but can produce uneven sky values in the photograph—especially with strong blue-absorbing filters.

Subject contrast relates to the difference of the reflectance of the various surfaces and the difference in the illumination of the sunlit and shadowed areas. Shadowed areas in which we wish to preserve the impression of substance and texture, and high-value areas in which we wish to preserve the impression of substance, texture and light, constitute the limits of the *textural range*. From the first step of value above full black to the first step of value below pure white constitutes the *dynamic range* (usually two or more stops or Zones greater than the textural range). The effective exposure scale of the film relates more to the textural range than to the dynamic range and our problem, in most cases, is to relate the subject contrast range to the textural range of the film. This contrast situation is handled differently with different materials, as we will see later on.

COLOR PHOTOGRAPHY (CONVENTIONAL)

Comment herein relates in the main to *positive* color film (such as Kodachrome), rather than to negative color film (such as Ektacolor). Negative color film has a somewhat greater exposure range as prints therefrom are subject to some control in contrast and color values. The subject of color-printing is beyond the scope of this article. Positive color film has a much shorter exposure range than most black-and-white film (excepting some Polaroid Land materials). Ideally, the subject should be illuminated in flat light—either sunlight or skylight (the latter may require a correction

filter). Under such lighting the total range of diffuse reflectances will not exceed a range of about 1 to 48 (black velvet reflects about 2% and white chalk about 96%). As such extremes are seldom found in nature we may say that the average colorful subject in flat light does not exceed a 1 to 25 contrast range. This relates to 5½ stops or Zones, inclusive. If we include a standard gray card (18% reflectance) in this typical subject, and place the luminance of the card on Zone V, *all the other subject values will fall on their appropriate Zone of the exposure scale.* Exposing any color above or below its optimum position on the exposure scale will of course result in a lightening or darkening of the color in reference to its "normal" value. For esthetic and emotional reasons we often vary our exposures to achieve colors and values more appropriate to what we feel about the subject and what we wish to express.

If our subject is illuminated so that we have *both* sunlit and shadowed areas it presents a considerably increased contrast scale. With a relatively soft sunlit-shadowed ratio—say 1 to 4—our basic 1 to 25 contrast range becomes a 1 to 100 contrast range; the color film cannot compress this range into its effective textural exposure range and something must yield. Shadows may be rendered too deep, or high values will be "burned-out." Depending upon the relative importance of these areas the photographer must make decisions favoring one extreme or the other, using fill-in light if possible, or re-visualizing and re-composing his picture to better relate the values of the scene to the exposure scale of the film.

If we consider the ARROW of the Weston Scale (Zone V) as representing middle gray, the "A" (Zone IV) and the "C" (Zone VI) represent the limits of the *accurate* rendition of color subjects of about 9%, and 36% reflectance. Zone V represents 18%. At Zone VII (one Zone or stop above "C") we approach the high limit of color and texture rendition; at Zone VII½ we have reached it. Beyond Zone VII½ we will have burn-out—blank, colorless and textureless areas in the picture.

We can drop to Zone III (one Zone or stop below "A") and retain some impression of color—appropriate for low-value subjects of about 4 or 5% reflectance. Below Zone III a very dark image obtains, with very little color and texture. The scale terminates at practically total black at about Zone II.

With positive color film, expose to favor the desired quality of the high values unless the shadowed areas are of dominant interest.

Very early or very late in the day the light is "warm" (yellowish or reddish) and light-balancing filters of the 82 series will be helpful. In shade, or at high altitudes the light will be "cold" (bluish) and light-balancing filters of the 81 series are useful. The Kodak Skylight filter is helpful in most landscape work—at all times except after sunrise or near sunset. Color film made for artificial light can be used in daylight with the proper conversion filter (#85B for example with Type B Ektachrome).

COLOR PHOTOGRAPHY (POLAROID POLACOLOR LAND FILM)

The instructions for the use of Polacolor Land Film should be carefully followed. Polacolor is available in rolls (Type 48) and packs (Type 108) and in the 4 x 5 format (Type 58). Type 108 fits the #100 Polaroid Land camera. Temperature must be considered in terms of both exposure and development times. *Be sure to read the sections on temperature in the instructions packed with each roll or filmpack (or 4 x 5 packets) of Polacolor.* Polacolor film must be protected as much as possible from the effects of heat and humidity!

The Polacolor process has a rewarding exposure range and the colors are soft rather than garish. The policy of the manufacturer is to favor an esthetic balance of color rather than an effect of excessive brilliance and questionable "realism." Flesh tones have been carefully considered and the present color balance of Polacolor is related primarily to these values. It is too early to make decisive comment on how to relate this new material to the Hawaiian scene. I would assume that certain UV filters are indicated because of the general atmospheric conditions. It is also possible that a light magenta compensating filter, such as Kodak CC 0.5M or CC 1.0M, would be helpful in an environment dominated by the warm greens of the Hawaiian foliage.

We do not have as much control with Polacolor as with black-and-white or conventional color materials. Exposure, as with all color film, is more critical than with black-and-white film. Shorter or longer development times (in relation to the normal time which is determined by the temperature) will result in warmer (redder) or colder (bluer) images.

The automatic #100 Polaroid Land camera does well at the realistic level. The photographer can modify exposures over a three-stop range by adjusting the "lighten-darken" control dial on the shutter. With low-contrast subjects (irrespective of high or low luminance) this dial will be set in the "lighten" range. With high-contrast subjects the "darken" range may be used. Automatic as the camera is in principle and operation, it nevertheless allows the photographer a rewarding amount of control.

BLACK-AND-WHITE PHOTOGRAPHY (CONVENTIONAL)

References will be found in the Bibliography (Page 98) to works which offer descriptions of techniques, including the Zone System approach. We have in Hawaii the peculiar and sometimes perverse problem of managing a "soft" landscape to produce "strong" and convincing images. We do not achieve the impression of brilliancy and light by effecting mere *contrast*. Many pictures of Hawaii are harsh and bleak and fail to suggest the quality of soft glowing light which is such an important element of the Hawaiian experience. To achieve this quality we must try to keep the shadows luminous (implying adequate exposure), and the highlights likewise luminous and of delicate texture. Specular reflections (sun-glint on water and the shining edges of leaves, etc.) should be rendered pure white and not in conflict with too-light diffuse values of high-value subjects. If scintillations are to be convincing in the print the surrounding diffuse values should not be higher than Value VII—preferably Value VI or VI½. Esthetically, I believe that the preservation of textures and the sense of substance in the high-value areas is more important than the retention of these values in the dark areas. Scintillations are usually a very important characteristic of the subject and must be convincingly revealed.

In the print all areas of the image which are devoid of texture or "detail" (represented in the negative by areas of no appreciable density) should be rendered as rich, solid black. A gray rendition of an "empty" area is weak and distressing. Negatives should be so exposed and developed that important shadowed areas are represented by printable densities (with perhaps some small areas which can be printed as solid black and will give some vitality to the full print scale). The "Golden Rule" of black-and-white photography is this: Expose for the shadow values and develop for the high values. In simpler terms: Give more-than-normal exposure and less-than-normal development for subjects of average high contrast, and for low-contrast subjects, give less-than-normal exposure and more-than-normal development.

BLACK-AND-WHITE PHOTOGRAPHY (POLAROID LAND FILM)

After opening boxes of the 4 x 5 Polaroid Land film (Types 52, 57 and 55 P/N) be sure to keep the packets in the plastic bags provided with each box. Keep the end of the bag turned under to keep out humidity.

Polacolor prints do not require coating, but all other Polaroid Land print material does. Coat as soon as possible after processing. Under humid conditions the prints may take a very long time to thoroughly dry; hence avoid stacking the prints or allowing anything to come in contact with them (including fingertips!) until they are completely dry. Protect from dust, spray, rain or mist while drying. Superficial marks and finger prints can be covered by re-coating (but scratches will result if sand or grit or solidified specks of coating material are attached to the dried first coating).

If the high values of the print seem a little depressed, we can delay coating for an hour or more (depending upon atmospheric conditions) as the print will bleach on exposure to air. The highest values bleach first; prints should be watched to avoid over-bleaching. At the proper stage the prints can be coated and permanency assured.

Polaroid Land films Types 42 and 52 are quite vigorous in scale and are well suited to average Hawaiian subjects in flat sunlight or shade. For subjects of higher contrast Types 47, 57 and 107 (the 3000-speed film (in my experience 4000 ASA in daylight!) are suggested. Except with Type 107 used in the #100 Polaroid Land camera the other types will require a Neutral Density filter under normal daylight illumination (strong filters such as the "A" and "B" will effectively reduce the film speed from 4000 to 500). The N.D. filter of 1.20 density has a factor of 16x and will reduce the speed of the film to 250 ASA.

The very high speed of this material makes possible the use of small stops (favoring great depth-of-field) at the higher shutter speeds which are useful with pictures of fast-moving water and spray. Likewise, in the rain forests great depth-of-field and short exposures are possible and exciting pictures at dawn, dusk and even in moonlight can be made. Filters and/or the polarizer will effectively lower the film speed. For example, the polarizer (3x) with the 58 "B" (8x) combine with an exposure factor of 24x. The green filter alone would reduce the speed to 500 ASA. In the rain forest on a sunless day, the near foliage might read 25 c/ft². Placed on Zone V at 500 ASA speed this would require 1/25 sec at f/22 or 1/50 sec at f/16 with Type 47 or Type 57 film. While the recommended developing time is 10 seconds, the film will respond with increased contrast up to about 30 or 40 seconds developing time. The "normal" developing time is lessened as the temperature rises.

Used with the #100 Polaroid Land camera, the high speed of the Type 107 film is managed by the electronic shutter and no exposure control by the use of filters, etc., is required.

With Polaroid Land film the use of strong filters does not increase the basic contrast of the picture as it often does with conventional film, but the *separations* of values and the clarifying of distant textures and values by the reduction of haze gives the impression of increased contrast and brilliance. Fortunately, with the Polaroid Land films, the effects of filters can be checked on the spot.

Type 55 P/N Polaroid Land film is, for the serious photographer, perhaps the most rewarding material. His negative is secured on the spot, with the print serving, at least, as a proof. At present, Type 55 P/N film must be immersed in an 18% solution of sodium sulfite as soon as possible after processing (pulling through the rollers). Constant agitation is advised for 15 to 30 seconds; the negative remains in this solution for 4 or 5 minutes and then can be transferred to a tank of plain water for storage. At the end of the day, the negatives should be washed for 15 minutes or so, put through Photo-flo, and hung up to dry. Small splash-proof tanks are available from the Insul-8 Corporation, San Carlos, California, which greatly simplifies the procedure in the field with this film. This treatment in the sulfite solution can be done in full daylight.

The present effective speed of the Type 55 P/N film is ASA 64 for the optimum print, and ASA 32 for the optimum negative. The negative has fine quality and extraordinary fineness of grain; it has a moderately long exposure range—a textural range of about 1 to 16 (Zones III to VII inclusive at ASA 32). Because of the fact that we cannot change the negative density to any appreciable extent by different development times, the contrast of the *subject* determines the contrast of the printing papers to be used. With average subjects I have had good results with Kodabromide No. 4 and Ansco #120 print developer (which contains only Metol or Elon as the developing agent), using a diffused-light source in the enlarger.

In the preceding paragraphs we have discussed some basic technical facts. We cannot attempt to write about the creative potential of the individual—what he might see, feel and execute. The vision and the system of one photographer may be incomprehensible to another. The basic aspects of Hawaii are there for all to savor; the geology, zoology, botany, ecology, anthropology, art and society, and the sheer pleasure of living in a beautiful land all constitute an impressive range of subject material for photographers of every kind and persuasion. The potentials for creative photography in Hawaii are enormous. It may at times be difficult to break through the conventional concepts and applied techniques in their relation to the ordinary impressions of Hawaii, but once the photographer identifies himself with the realities of the area and establishes confidence in what he sees and desires to interpret, a new world of beauty and exciting experience opens wide for him.

A.A.

LIST OF PLATES

Authentic Books on HAWAII and PHOTOGRAPHY

Alexander, W. D. *A Brief History of the Hawaiian People*. New York: American Book Company, 1891.

Allen, Gwenfread. *Hawaii's War Years 1941-1945*. Honolulu: University of Hawaii Press, 1950.

Beckwith, Martha W. *Hawaiian Mythology*. New Haven: Yale University Press, 1940.

Buck, Peter H. (Te Rangi Hiroa). *Arts and Crafts of Hawaii*. Honolulu: Bishop Museum Press, 1957.

———. *Vikings of the Sunrise*. New York: J. B. Lippincott Company, 1938.

Bryan, E. H., Jr. *The Hawaiian Chain*. Honolulu: Bishop Museum Press, 1954.

Day, A. Grove. *Hawaii and Its People*. New York: Duell, Sloan and Pearce, 1960.

Day, A. Grove, and Stroven, Carl. *A Hawaiian Reader*. New York: Appleton-Century-Crofts, Inc., 1959.

Ellis, William. *Narrative of a Tour of Hawaii, or Owhyhee; with Remarks on the History, Traditions, Manners, Customs and Language of the Inhabitants of the Sandwich Islands*. Originally printed in London in 1827. Reprinted Honolulu: Advertiser Publishing Company, Ltd., 1963.

Gosline, William A. and Brock, Vernon E. *Handbook of Hawaiian Fishes*. Honolulu: University of Hawaii Press, 1960.

Halford, John Francis. *9 Doctors & God*. Honolulu: University of Hawaii Press, 1954.

Joesting, Edward and Adams, Ansel (photographs). *The Islands of Hawaii*. Honolulu: Bishop National Bank of Hawaii (now the First National Bank of Hawaii), 1958.

Korn, Alfons L. *The Victorian Visitors*. Honolulu: University of Hawaii Press, 1953.

Kuck, Loraine E. and Tongg, Richard C. *Hawaiian Flowers and Flowering Trees*. Tokyo, Japan and Rutland, Vermont: Charles E. Tuttle Company, 1958.

Kuykendall, Ralph S. *The Hawaiian Kingdom 1778-1854*. Honolulu: University of Hawaii Press, 1938.

———. *The Hawaiian Kingdom 1854-1874*. Honolulu: University of Hawaii Press, 1953.

Lind, Andrew W. *Hawaii's People*. Honolulu: University of Hawaii Press, 1955.

Malo, David. *Hawaiian Antiquities*. Honolulu: Bishop Museum Press, 1951.

Munro, George C. *Birds of Hawaii*. Tokyo, Japan and Rutland, Vermont: Bridgeway Press, 1960.

Stearns, Harold T. *Geology of the Hawaiian Islands*. (Bulletin 8, Prepared in cooperation with the Geological Survey, United States Department of the Interior.) Honolulu: Territory of Hawaii, 1946.

Adams, Ansel. *Making a Photograph*. London and New York: Studio Publications, 1935-1943.

———. *Basic Photo Series*. New York: Morgan and Morgan.
   I. *Camera and Lens* (a revised edition in preparation), 1964.
   II. *The Negative*, 1962 (3rd printing).
   III. *The Print*, 1964 (6th printing).
   IV. *Natural-light Photography*, 1963 (4th printing).
   V. *Artificial-light Photography*, 1962 (2nd printing).

———. *Polaroid Land Photography Manual*. New York: Morgan and Morgan, 1963.

———. *These We Inherit*. San Francisco: Sierra Club, 1962. *The Parklands of America*.

———. *Exposure Record*. New York: Morgan and Morgan, 1945 et seq.

Carroll, John S. *Photo-Lab-Index*. New York: Morgan and Morgan, 1964 et seq.

Newhall, Beaumont. *The History of Photography*. New York: Museum of Modern Art, 1937-1964.

Newhall, Beaumont and Nancy. *Masters of Photography*. New York: George Braziller, 1958.

Newhall, Nancy. *This is the American Earth*. San Francisco: Sierra Club, 1960.

———. *Death Valley* (Ansel Adams photographs). San Francisco: 5 Associates, Inc. 1954.

———. *Mission San Xavier del Bac* (Ansel Adams photographs). San Francisco: 5 Associates, Inc., 1954.

———. *Yosemite Valley* (edited; photographs by Ansel Adams). San Francisco: 5 Associates, Inc., 1959.

———. *Monograph: Ansel Adams*. San Francisco: de Young Memorial Museum, 1963 (in conjunction with the Ansel Adams Retrospective Exhibition, 1923-1963).

———. *The Eloquent Light* (Vol. 1, Ansel Adams Biography). San Francisco: Sierra Club, 1963.

➤➤➤➤➤➤➤➤➤➤➤➤➤➤➤➤◄◄◄◄◄◄◄◄◄◄◄◄◄◄◄◄

Book design and end-paper maps by Leo Holub.
Black and white photo-engravings by the Walter J. Mann Co.
Color plates, printing and complete production
supervision by H. S. Crocker Co., Inc.
Binding by The Cardoza Bookbinding Co.

COVER PHOTOGRAPH: *Coastline near Nanakuli, west shore of Oahu*

HANALEI

Waimea Canyon

WAIMEA · LIHUE

Kauai

Niihau

Oah—

WAHIAWA

KANEOHE · KAU—

PEARL HARBOR

· HONOLULU

Waikiki Beach

The Principal Islands of

HAWAII

The islands of Hawaii are a group of volcanic peaks stretching for some 1500 nautical miles in a nearly east-west direction across the northern Tropic Zone of the Pacific Ocean. There are eight major islands in the chain, comprising what is generally thought of as the Hawaiian Islands, all of which lie in the eastern third of the group. Seven of these islands are inhabited, the only exception being the low, dry island of Kahoolawe. Two thousand ninety-one miles south-west of San Francisco lies the capital city of Honolulu on the island of Oahu.